HOW TO INVEST IN SHARES?

Essentials of Investments

Dr. Sriram Ananthan

ABOUT THE AUTHOR

How many times have you had to give up on a lifelong dream just because you thought you did not have the resources or skills needed to achieve them? How often do you let your circumstances define what your short- and long-term future will turn out to be? If you are like any other individual, chances are that you may be hiding your greatest dream and desires all the way in the back of the last drawer, never to see the light of day.

I used to be like this, living with a passive attitude, letting the tides of life shape my present and what was to become of me. I worked a 9 to 5 job at a bank for the longest time, doing the same thing over and over again and actually being able to learn and grow in the marketing field. But something deep inside me always knew that I could be doing so much more- so much more of what my heart has always wanted to achieve.

So, I took the chance, put on my hiking boots, and prepared to straddle the hills of struggle no matter what it took. Thirteen years later, I have finally conquered my fears and doubts and am ready to share my experience of immersing myself in the world of business development and entrepreneurship with young professionals like me who just need that little bit of a nudge of motivation to get them going.

I am Dr. Sriram Ananthan from Canada, and I am an entrepreneur, coach, leader, speaker, writer, and, most importantly, a friend. What I aim to do with my knowledge and experience is to channel it all towards creating a well-rounded experience for anyone who needs guidance to get their professional lives on track.

TABLE OF CONTENTS

INTRODUCTION

Everyone has some goals in his/her life. Some are short-term while others are long-term goals. In today's era, there is a greater need to put aside a portion of your income in order to achieve these life's goals which may include a wedding, children's education, retirement planning, or buying a house. Some of us succeed to attain these goals while many of us fail to realize, if not all, many goals of their lives. The question is, "how some of us fruitfully accomplish their life's goals?" The answer is very simple; through "financial planning". It is very important to have a plan in order to conquer any goal. The importance of having plan is expressed by a French writer, Antoine de Saint-Exupery as, "A goal without a plan is just a wish". Warren Buffet, one of the most prominent investor, laid emphasis on the prominence of planning and quoted as, "Someone is sitting in a shade today because someone planted a tree a long time ago". An intelligent plan requires you to put your money in suitable mix of assets that allow you to return a potential income so that you may achieve your financial goals. Money invested wisely can maximize your earnings on given investments.

There exists several opportunities for investment and you may follow a herd while making an investment decision. But this is not a strategy of an intelligent investor. A wise investor is the one who can make use of logical piece of information to check for appropriate facts and opportunities prior to making an investment decision.

As stated earlier, various investment opportunities are available to accomplish your financial goals but the best is the one that can maximize your return on investments. One of those investments options is investing through "stock exchange" directly or indirectly by buying the shares of listed companies.

This book is designed to give you an insight about essential concepts involved in the field of investments. This valuable understanding will enable its reader to make several investment decisions during the course of his/her life.

The objective of this text is very simple and clear; to help readers gain a meaningful but fundamental knowledge about (1) investment opportunities in stock market, (2) making intelligent investment decisions, and (3) recognizing the issues concerning investments in shares.

If you are looking to create a strong financial plan to attain your life's goals. It will cover all the fundamental concepts from defining a share to investment options available to opening an account with broker and finally some potential tips to generate superior returns on your investment. Because the first step of anything starts from learning:

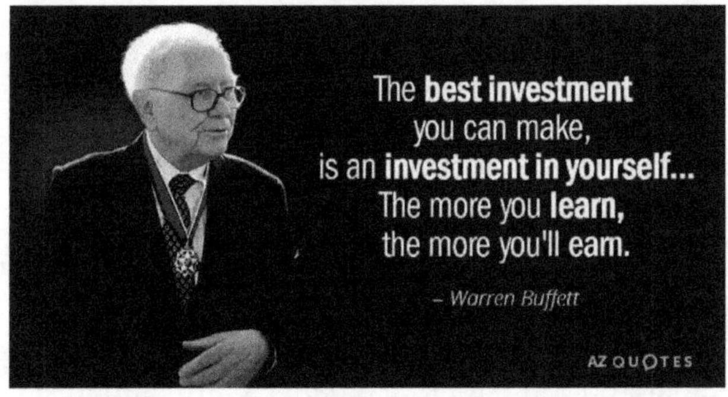

CHAPTER ONE
WHAT ARE SHARES?

If you are fresh to the universe of investing in stock market, you may not have knowledge of shares. Therefore, it is very important to have the understanding of shares at first place. A share may be defined as:

*"A proportionate stake in the equity of a corporation is represented by shares. We can also term them as **equity securities.** "*

Who issues shares?

Shares are issued by corporations listed on stock exchange. For a company to issue shares, they must have a registration at stock exchange. Companies which are registered on stock exchanges are called "Listed companies".

Motives behind issuing shares

In contrast to borrowing funds from outsiders, companies have an option to rise outside capital by selling or issuing shares, in order to finance their wide operations. One of the way by which company raises capital in the form of equity is by selling (issuing) shares in the market. This permits investor to buy share from the company at a certain price. By buying at least single share of a company, an investor is entitled to become a shareholder of the same company and this gives him the right to share a portion of company's income as profit, known as dividend.

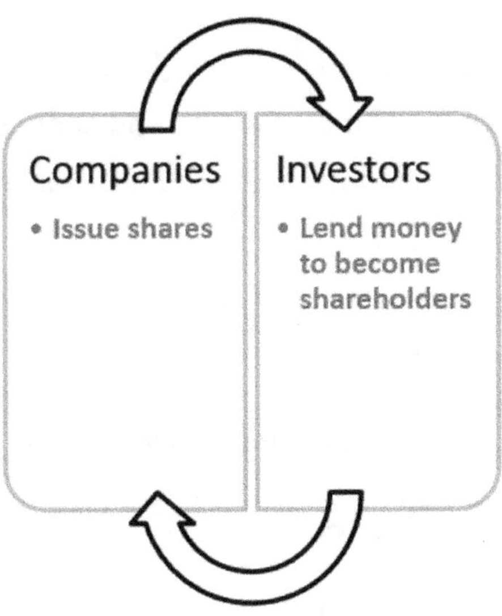

Figure 1: Offering of securities to investors

- ## **Initial Public offerings (IPOs)**

A process through which a company issues or sells its securities for the very first time to general public is called initial public offerings (IPO). There are several reasons for a company to go for IPOs which include raising capital for a targeted project; or listing securities on stock exchange; or fulfilling debt obligations; or meeting working capital requirements etc.

Characteristics of equity securities

There are two types of equity securities issued by corporations i.e. preferred shares and common shares (or common stock). These shares are characterized on the basis of special features attached to them. Followings are the characteristics or feature which differential one security to another:

- Face value (or Par Value)

- Life of a security

- Voting rights

- Cash flow rights.

Face Value

Face value (also known as par value) is the value of a share which is stated on it. This signifies the original value attached to a share. However, companies are legally allowed to issue share at the price different than its face value.

Life of a security

The time period for which securities are allowed to hold by its holder is called life of a security. It may range from a few days to years, or even infinite period. Some equity securities are issued with maturity dates but most of them are issued for indefinite period of time.

Voting Rights

There are certain shares which carry special rights called voting rights attached to them. A holder of these shares can exercise these rights, upon its buying. These shareholders participate in major decisions/events of the companies through their voting rights. These important decisions include; electing board of directors; or mergers and acquisition; or discontinuing business operations; or any important decisions other than managing a day-to-day business matters.

Cash Flow Rights

This represents the rights of shareholders to claim such distributions as dividends. Dividends are the profits distributed to shareholders out of company's total earnings of a period.

When a company is at the brink of bankruptcy or liquidity, assets are distributed in the order of priority to claim, or *seniority ranking*.

Types of equity securities

The two main types of equity securities include preferred shares (also known as preferred stock) and common shares (also called ordinary shares or common stocks). Companies may also issue/offer warrants and convertible bonds, on top of it. Let's discuss briefly both of these types of equity securities:

Preferred Shares

Preferred shares are said so because holders of this securities are given preference while distributing dividends. They are also given priority on claiming company's assets in contrast to common shareholders in the case of liquidation of assets. In short, owners of preferred shares are given partiality in most of the cases.

In contrast to above, preferred shareholders are not eligible for voting rights in the company. They are also not residual claimants on the assets of the company, in the case of liquidation.

Preferred shares contain par value along with dividend stated as a percentage of par value, stated on it. Thus, the amount of dividend is fixed and does not change during the course of its life. However, company is not legally bound to set aside a portion of its income for the distribution of its dividend. It depends upon the financial performance of a company. If a company is performing poorly during a period, the board of directors may not approve their dividend in that period.

The amount of dividend of a single share is calculated by multiplying dividend rate with its par value. For example, dividend amount on 10%, $100 preferred share will be calculated as:

$$\text{Dividend amount} = \text{Par Value} \times \text{Dividend Rate}$$

$$= \$100 \times 10\%$$

$$= \$10 \text{ per share}$$

Preferred shares may also contain some pre-specified terms upon issuance. For example, they can also be bought back by the issuer at the pre-determined price which may or may not be equal to its face value. The price at which a preferred share is bought back is called its redemption price.

Another classification of preferred shares is based upon the policy of dividends being unpaid in the previous periods e.g. cumulative and non-cumulative. Cumulative preferred shares needed to be paid in full for any unpaid dividend (promised but not paid in the past) prior to distributing any dividends to common shareholders. On the other hand, non-cumulative preferred shares do not need to pay for any unpaid dividends before proceeding dividend payments to common shareholders. In the case of liquidation, however, preferred shareholders represent a superior claim for any missed dividends prior to the distribution made to common shareholders.

Common Share

Common share (generally referred to as common stocks, voting shares or ordinary shares) is the chief type of equity securities offered/issued by companies. Likewise preferred stock, it also represents the ownership stake in a company. Common shares are issued for indefinite period of time. This means that they do not have any maturity attached with them. They typically have a face value which may be as low as 1 cent per share in USA. Their market value is independent of the face value. For example, a common share with a face value of 1 cent may be sold to the investor for $100.

The greater proportion of equity securities is comprised of common shares. There are several common shareholders of large companies representing a significant proportion in the total shares of those companies. Investors have a choice of trading the shares of public or private limited companies. Public limited companies offer shares which are traded on stock exchange. A stock exchange is a place for buying and selling of securities of listed companies. It is a place that facilitates trading of shares among sellers and buyers. In contrast to this, private limited companies do not offer their shares for trading on stock exchange.

Common stock signifies voting rights and cash flow rights depending upon the number and value of shares an investor owns. They have a right to vote in the important affairs of the companies; and rights to be paid a portion of company's profit every year, called shareholder's cash flow rights. The distribution of portion of profit to shareholders of a company is called dividend. The amount of dividends is determined by board of directors in annual general meeting (AGM) and is depends upon company's performance. If the performance of a company is poor, the board of directors is often reluctant to pay any dividend in a certain period. However, the board of directors may pay a maximum amount of dividend in a year in which company's performance is very good. Thus, a common shareholder may enjoy a good earning in that year.

They have a residual claim on the company's assets and earning, in an event of liquidation. This implies that they are the last one to claim on the assets of the company and are paid only when the payments of higher seniority is being satisfied.

How do shares work?

Shares represents ownership stake in a corporation. By buying shares of a company, you become a shareholder of that company and you can claim on company's earnings and assets. Sometime, you are also granted with some special rights such as voting rights.

Let's take an example to elaborate this: consider a company having capital of $10,000 divided into 1000 shares of $10 each, and you have purchased 50 shares of it. You would hold 5% ownership stakes in that company.

How can you participate in stock market?

There comes some occasions that many people have to participate in stock markets either directly, by buying shares of the companies listed on stock exchange, or by indirectly, by taking part in retirement plan or mutual funds (explained later in chapter). It docs not matter whether someone has bought shares or not, most of the people are well aware of the stock market because of the information about stock market indices are reported most widely in news and advertisements. Stock market indices exhibits shares performances in a group and are considered useful indicators of the economy.

You can also contribute to overall economic progress by participating in shares market. Share market provides access to the investors by opening an account with brokers (explained in later chapter). Thus, brokers provide you an immediate link with the market by maintaining an account. The direct buying and selling of shares is happened through them.

Motives behind investing in shares

The prime reason for investing in shares of any kind is to build a personal financial track for the future. The fact is that individuals work to build the wealth of some kind which may consist of value of their assets, or services in the place of market. Majority individuals have to encounter some investment decisions in order to accomplish some specific financial goals. They strive to create some wealth during the course of their working period mostly through investing.

Retirement Decisions

- To supplement the retirement income, people try to create different sources. According to an estimate, less than half of the households headed by individuals aging between 47 and 62 and if they cease their working, they will not be able to supplement their retirement income significantly. In addition to this, their retirement income will fall below poverty line.

- There are two types of retirement plans which are offered to employees i.e. defined contribution plan and defined benefit plans. A defined contribution plan is a self-managed plan where employees have to contribute a defined amount towards a retirement income. Whereas in defined benefit plan, a definite amount of money is provided every month upon retirement.

- A defined contribution plan has been revolutionized and re-defined now days. The emphasis is on choosing various investment alternatives such as stocks, bonds, or investment contracts, in order to supplement the retirement income. There are many choice and directly effects the retirement benefits. In the past, employees were not really concerned about the investment decisions concerning retirement plans but future employees will have to do so.

- Out of all investment alternative discussed a while ago, investment in shares offer a volatile but superior returns to the investors. But how does it work? Consider a self-managed retirement plan, the Individual Retirement Account (IRA). IRA is a major technique used by Americans to provide for their retirement income. The funds in this account may be invested for as long as 40 years. Suppose, an individual is contributing $1,000 annually in this account. The funds in the account could be invested in shares and other investment alternatives at the compound interest rate. Suppose, investment in the shares of a particular company offers average return of 10% p.a. whereas other investment alternatives (including bonds and/or contracts etc.) yield 5% return compounded annually. Following table will illustrate you the importance of investing your funds wisely in a retirement plan.

Annual Investment in IRA	Time period (In years)	Future Value of annual investment compounded annual at:	
		5%	10%
$1,000	20	$33,067	$57,275
$1,000	40	$120,800	$442,593

Creating wealth for life time

On top of matters concerning retirement plans, individuals' motives for investing in stocks is to seek superior return on given level of risk. Increasing return by directly owning shares of the companies help them to build wealth for their lifetime.

Factors affecting investment decisions

Each investor has its own financial resources and plans. Thus, there are many factors unique to the investors. Key factors which are common to all investors include:

- Requirement of return

- Risk tolerance

- Time period

Requirement of return

There are two components of return i.e. capital gain / loss and yield. Capital gain is defined as appreciation or depreciation in the price of an asset over a period of time whereas yield is the income part of that asset. For example, if a stock is bought for $100 a year ago and sold for $110 now and yield $5 of dividend, then total return of that stock would be:

Total Return = Capital Gain / (Loss) + Yield

= (110-100) + 5

= 10+5

Total Return = $15

% Total Return = Total Return / Purchase

Price x 100

$$= 15/100 \text{ x } 100$$

$$= 0.15 \text{ x } 100$$

$$= 15\%$$

On the basis of age of an investor, a financial advisor may suggest him to earn 10% rate of return to meet his or her financial goal of creating a portfolio worth of $1,000,000 at the time of retirement. If the probability of meeting this goal seems difficult for an investor, then he may be additionally advised to consider other factors such as saving levels and supplementary income to adjust for it.

It is up to investor what perspective he/she counts to consider return. For some, total-perspective is important while others may consider capital gain, or income. Investors who are total-return-oriented do not count sources of returns like capital gain and income. Alternatively, investors may consider income and capital gains as equally importance to meet their long-term needs.

The return requirement, for long-term investments, normally quoted in real terms, which implies adjustments for inflation. Inflation decreases the purchasing power of an individual. Therefore, he needs to be well informed about the return he will get in real terms. An investment whose return increases more than increase in inflation rate is consider best and increase the spending power of an investor.

Risk Tolerance

Risk tolerance is the function of two factors i.e. ability to take risk and willingness to take risk.

The ability to take risk depends upon the balance among assets and liabilities. If an investor has more in assets than liabilities, then his life style may not be affected by loss resulting from taking risk.

Willingness to accept risk is defined by investor's psychology, which may be assessed by undergoing few tests conductor by psychologists.

There are certain situations in which investor's ability and willingness to take risk might alter. In such situation, an investor must seek an advice from expert financial investment advisor to determine the suitable risk level he/she may take by investing in stocks.

Time Period

The investor must define the time period during which an investment should generate a required return. Depending upon the financial needs of an investor, investment could be done for the period of short term period as well as for the period of long term.

For an example, an investor who wants to buy a new home or new car or to pay for educational fee in three to four years will need funds in shorter time period as compare to an investor who is planning for retirement in 25 years or more.

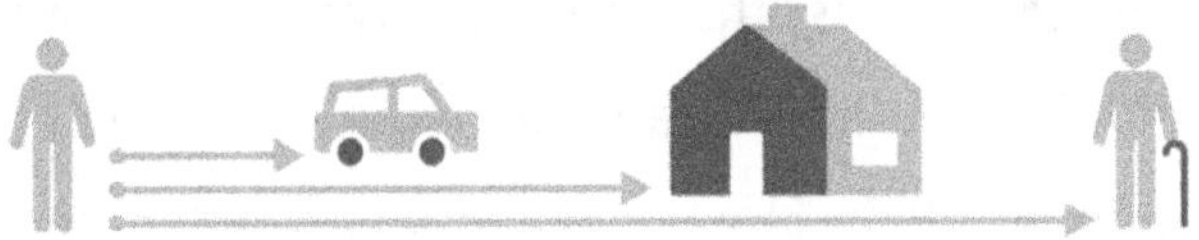

Figure 2: Planning for Future

CHAPTER TWO
STOCK EXCHANGES AND BROKERS

As you have prepared yourself to invest your money in shares, you realize that most people you have certainly heard of the New York Stock Exchange, but you don't know about its working. It should be a matter of concern for you whether the stock you buy trade there or not? Have you heard about the speculation losses, when there was bubble in NASDAQ market in the year 2000? When someone says e-communication is the fate of investment, but you really don't have any idea of it. Even more basics, like drop in 10 points in Dow-Jones 30 index, what does that tell you?

Significance of Financial Markets

Corporations save a reasonable amount of time by investing capital that is beyond their capacity. This investment is done in expanding business operations. In the same way, governments have to borrow great amount of capital to finance their capital projects. By the virtue of financial markets, both business and government raise the funds needed by them, by issuing their securities. At the same time, financial markets permits investor to invest their excess funds in the securities issued in the market, in order to earn a return on it.

Financial markets contribute effectively in bringing welfare to the overall economy. Their main purpose is to channel funds from lenders to borrowers.

The Primary Markets

It is a market for seeking funds by selling new securities to the investors (buyers). Fresh sales of Treasury bonds, or Nestle stock, or corporate bonds take place in the primary markets.

When a corporation issues its shares for the very first time, it is called **initial public offerings (IPOs).** IPOs are issued in the market with the assistance of investment bankers. IPOs, once taken up by investors, trade further in secondary markets repeatedly. IPOs, once sold by corporations, cannot be bought back.

Following figure will illustrate the functioning of primary markets:

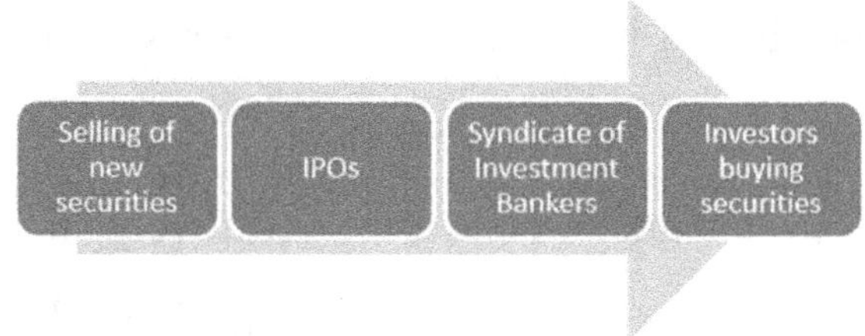

Figure 3: Functioning of primary markets

Investment Bankers

Issuers depend upon investment bankers to utilize their expertise along with their capacity to reach potential investors. They are specialized in designing and selling fresh securities in the primary markets while extending their services for secondary markets as well. Some of the major investment banking names includes Goldman Sachs, JP Morgan, and Morgan Stanley.

The process by which investment bankers acquire securities from a firm with an aim of reselling it to public is called underwriting. This is the reason why investment bankers are also called underwriters. While accepting (purchasing) securities from the issuers, they assume all of the risk of reselling to investors. The issuer gets benefit at this stage by receiving the required funds in the form of check, to spend for the purpose of which funds are being raised.

Investment bankers, usually form a syndicate or group, in order to protect themselves against any potential loss. This is a very effect strategy of diversification.

Private Placements

Private placements represent a process by which new securities are issued directly to financial institutions such as pension funds and insurance companies. By doing so, companies saves a lot by avoiding registration cost at Securities and Exchange Commission (SEC) and investment bankers fee as they are not typically involved in private placements.

The Secondary Markets

After the successful issuance of IPOs by corporations in the primary markets, there should be an efficient mechanism for the resale of these securities if investors consider this an attractive opportunity. These existing securities are re-sold in a markets called ***secondary markets.***

"A markets for the trading of existing securities among investors are called secondary markets."

In secondary markets, transactions take place among investors only. Securities are sold to buyers by sellers on cash. The issuer receives no capital (or cash) in secondary markets transactions.

In addition to the trading of warrants, bonds and derivatives; secondary markets exists to provide transactions for common stocks and preferred stocks. Following figure will explain the basic secondary markets operations.

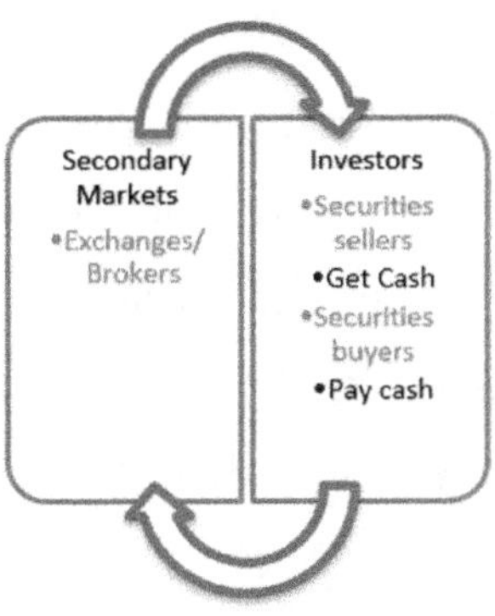

Figure 4: Basic operations of secondary markets

Trading Places

Securities are traded between investors in the secondary markets and therefore there is a need for trading venue-either electronically or physically-where orders can be placed between investors. **Orders** represent instructions by investors, who wish to trade, to providers of trading services, as for example brokers and deals, discussed later in this chapter.

Securities Exchanges

Securities exchanges (also known as exchanges) represent a place where traders interact with each other to trade securities. Only ***listed securities*** are traded on exchanges. Listed securities are issued by those companies who meet particular listing requirements of exchanges. In the past, these trades were negotiated by brokers and dealers on the floor of exchange. Today, dealers and brokers submit them the order electronically.

Exchanges provide various functions i.e. regulation of member's actions and regulation of issuers. Exchanges regulates members' actions by specifying the trading rules whereas issuers are regulated generally by requiring them timely issuance of financial statements and appropriate disclosure of matters. On top of this, exchanges also make sure the fact that companies are operated for the benefit of all shareholders not for a particular group of individuals. The regulatory authority is given by national or regional government, generally by drafting an agreements among members of exchanges and issuers.

In exchange of services provided to both issuers and investors, they charge fees. Fees is charged to the sellers, the buyers, or both participants.

The New York Stock Exchange

Dating back to 1792, the New York Stock Exchange (NYSE) is the earlier and distinguished secondary market in USA. It is one of the largest and valued equity market based upon the total market capitalization of listed securities. In the past, it was operated as private organization. However, a historical change happened when it became a public entity in the year 2005 resulting acquisition of Archipelago Exchange (ArcaEx), an electronic trading exchange. In 2007 it merged with Euronext, the biggest stock exchange in Europe, caused the formation of NYSE Euronext. In 2008, NYSE Euronext formed a merger with American Stock Exchange (termed as NYSE MKT), which is specialized in the trading of small companies efficiently.

Figure 5 Image Courtesy at "Yahoo.com"

NYSE is open for trading Monday to till Friday from 9:30 AM to 4:00 PM ET. However, stock exchange does not open for trading during federal holidays. The opening and closing of the stock exchange is marked with bells indicating a trading day. At 9:30 AM ET, the opening bell is rung and at 4:00 PM ET closing bell is rung – terminating trading for the day.

NYSE Trading

Trading at NYSE often executed in the form the large **blocks** by institutional investors. Each block constitutes at least 10,000 shares.

Program trading includes the trading of worth $1 million or more in the basket of 15 share or above. Program trading exhibits almost 30 percent of total volume of trading at NYSE in order to exploit the arbitrage opportunities among common stocks and options and index futures.

The OTC (Over-The-Counter) Market

Securities of the companies which are not listed on exchanges, are traded in the market called the OTC (Over-the-counter) market. And thus called OTC securities. These are the small companies who do not have enough capital to meet the requirement of exchanges. OTC securities are traded electronically and quoted on the Pink Sheets Electronic Quotation Service.

The investment in these companies is considered to be very risky, and may lead to substantial loss to the wealth of investors. These types of trading places are also alternative trading venues in USA and multilateral trading facilities in Europe.

CHAPTER THREE
WHERE AND HOW TO BUY SHARES

There are various manners by which you can take an interest in the financial exchange. The direct way is by purchasing and selling shares. The other is indirect way through an aggregate vehicle, wherein shares are assembled, for example, an Exchange Traded Funds (ETFs) or mutual funds.

MUTUAL FUNDS

During the 1990s, representatives started to accentuate another pattern in the closeout of burden common assets whereby they offer a few classes of fund's share, each with an alternate mix of front-end load (deals charge), yearly expense, and recovery expense. The thought is that if financial specialists are hesitant to pay higher deals charges when they purchase portions of a reserve, for instance, the merchants can do too by energizing not so much front but rather more in yearly and recovery expenses. All charges and costs must be expressed in the plan, and financial specialists should deliberately peruse a reserve's outline before contributing.

INSTRUCTIONS TO PURCHASE A SHARE

The six-advance intend to purchasing shares on the web are as follows:

- Locate a decent online merchant. Above all else, you have to locate a decent online representative. First you need to decide whether to experience an online business firm or through an up close and personal dealer.

- Open a speculation account.

- Transfer cash to your record.

- Locate a share you need to purchase. After assessing a share, choose the costs you'd like to buy at, so you realize whether to make a "market" or "constrained" request.

- Purchase the stock. To save money on dealer expenses, you can get a few stocks straightforwardly from the organization.

- Audit your offer positions consistently.

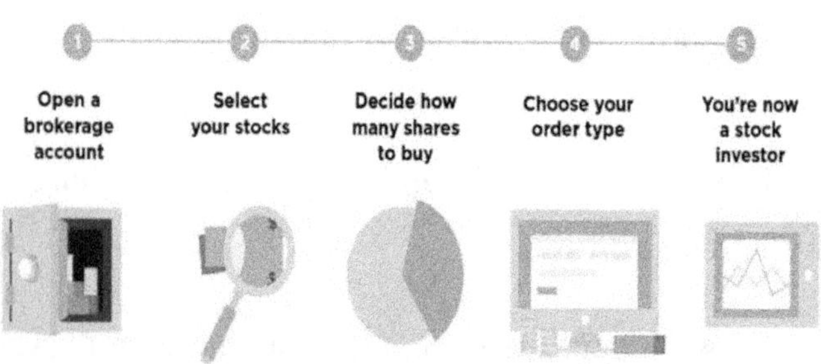

Figure 6 Basic steps of buying shares

How might you purchase and sell shares?

When you teach your agent to purchase shares, he/she purchases the offers for you at the best cost accessible at the time. Before the finish of day's exchanging, you will get an affirmation note. This demonstrates the subtleties of the exchange. Your merchant will demonstrate when he/she needs your cash to pay for the offers. You can purchase shares when an organization first comes to advertise - that is at buoyancy or privatization; or you can get them through the financial exchange once they are available for use and being exchanged. Organizations which are going to issue shares frequently promote in an everyday paper. In the event that you choose to purchase these offers, you can look for more data from the organization's site or you can top off the application structure at the partnered bank or approach the organization for an outline. Round out the application structure and submit it with your compensation request, at the bank. There is nothing more to pay. On the other hand, you can go to a stockbroker who will get them for you. Most offer dealings occur in what is known as the optional market.

This is the place existing investors sell and new financial specialists purchase. Today, purchasing offers is simple. You can purchase and sell shares by reaching a stockbroker, bank or speculation counsel, either face to face or over the web or phone.

How might you discover a stockbroker?

Stockbrokers today have a scope of administrations custom fitted for the requirements of the developing quantities of little investors. Some work from the Stock Trade Building, some from Rulers Street and other comparative areas around the city, and some just by phone. Most huge banks offer managing administrations too. Before picking a stockbroker, contact a few of them and ask the amount they will charge. They anticipate that you should contrast their charges and those of different intermediaries.

An individual financial specialist ought to pick a retail merchant, ideally one that meets his necessities as far as administrations required. When he comes up short on an opportunity to investigate individual organizations and stocks, at that point a full administration merchant is suggested. In picking a handle, the financial specialist should make sure that the intermediary is a Securities Broker of good remaining at the country's Stock Trade. It is significant that the financial specialist should believe his merchant and that he is fulfilled by the administrations it is giving him, for example, advertise reports, nature of counsel with respect to stock determination and timing of buys and deals, nature of exchange executions, on-time conveyance of significant records and different administrations.

BOOK BUILDING PROCEDURE FOR NEW ORGANIZATIONS

Book Building is the procedure of value disclosure and evaluating another offer issue. The procedure by which a financier endeavors to decide, at what cost to offer an Initial public offering dependent on interest from institutional speculators at its effective cost revelation dependent on real free market activity by educated speculators.

HOW MIGHT YOU CHOOSE WHICH OFFERS TO PURCHASE?

A stockbroker does purchasing and selling on his respectability accounts and for the benefit of his customers as people can't bargain for themselves in the market. A rundown of stockbrokers is accessible from the Stock Trade on country's Stock exchange. Stockbrokers offer an assortment of administrations yet in the event that you know precisely what you need, basically call the agent for an "execution just" administration and solicit them to purchase the offers from your decision. Stock exchange market offers three market portions. The first portion is the money market dependent on multi day clearing and repayment. Secondly Ceaseless Subsidizing framework where money market's net buys can be extended for another working days. Thirdly Deliverable Future Contracts enable financial specialists to buy or deal on a forward contract premise clearing and repayment of these agreement happens on last Friday of the months and new contract begins the next Monday Money Settled Future Contract where contract is for ninety days, yet speculator has a decision to go into any of the three gets that are constantly open for month's end expiry based of money repayment with underline money market cost of the scrip.

A stockbroker or money related guide can enable you to pick which offers to purchase, and exhortation on the best time to sell. You should choose:

- Will I need the cash soon?

- On the other hand, would you be able to leave you cash to develop over various years?

- Alternatively, do you need a mix of both?

- How a lot of cash would you be able to stand to contribute?

- Will you spread this over few offers, or a bigger number?

- Do you need to put straightforwardly in offers?

- Are you inspired by backhanded methods for contributing, through shut end Shared Assets or through Term Fund Endorsements accessible at the Stock Trade?

Moreover, in the wake of having trained your representative to purchase shares, the agent will draw up contract notes, which commonly are sent to your location or cell phone number inside next 24 hours. This will show subtleties of the exchange did for your benefit. At this stage you can sell your offers in the event that you wish. You are currently qualified for go to the organization's Annual General Meeting (AGM). Conversely with different investors, particularly delegates from the institutional financial specialists. Only one sizeable disinvestment could have a significant effect to the result of your general activity.

CHAPTER FOUR
INTRADAY AND DELIVERY

In the event that you put resources into offer markets, at that point you would have in all likelihood known about Warren Buffett, the best financial specialist ever. A portion of the offers in Warren Buffett's portfolio were grabbed right around 20-25 years prior. Yet, the vast majority of us dislike Warren Buffett and holding shares for quite a long time at a stretch isn't easier for all individuals.

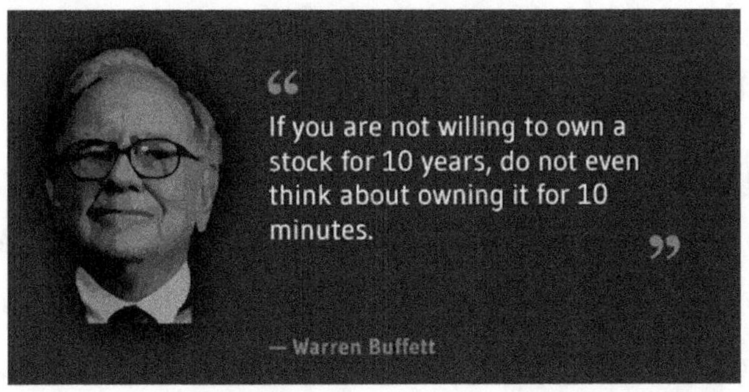

For the individuals who are not intrigued by long haul contributing or all the more explicitly delivery exchanging, there is an option as intra-day exchanging

hanging tight for them. What's more, this is where a great many little speculators attempt to make a fortune consistently, by following moment by moment change in offer costs.

WHAT IS INTRADAY AND DELIVERY EXCHANGING?

Person A and *Person B*, both exchange the value offer market. While *Person A* is an energetic merchant with marvelous broking skills, *Person B* is an amateur and needs to think about intraday exchanging.

Person A clarified:

Intraday exchanging suggests purchasing and selling protections around the same time.

Consistently, the cost of a security, state *XYZ* Company fluctuates. An intraday merchant benefits from this ascent or drop of value which offers colossal returns. Intraday brokers additionally get the advantage of edge subsidizing, whereby they can do exchanges of up to multiple times their record esteem which lifts their increases.

Intraday exchanging represents a danger of misfortune however there are measures to confine misfortunes. At whatever point *Person A* exchanges intraday, he screens the market intently and looks for guidance from Heavenly attendant Broking group of specialists. He likewise decides on stop misfortune which restrains his misfortunes to a base assuming any.

Like *Person A*, *Person B* is currently prepared to exchange intraday with Blessed messenger Broking.

Thus Intraday refers to all the purchasing/selling of offers happening inside one day, on another side, on the off chance that we purchase shares today and sell them following 1 day or 1 year then the sort of exchanging is called as Delivery Exchanging.

CONTRASTS BETWEEN INTRADAY EXCHANGING AND DELIVERY EXCHANGING

You can exchange two distinct courses in offer markets. You can either do intraday exchanging or you can decide on delivery based exchanging (venture). Intraday exchanging is regularly finished inside multi day – this implies you need to sell the offers that you have bought on that day prior to the end of business sectors. Regardless of whether you don't sell the offers independent from anyone else, they are naturally squared off before the end. Then again, in delivery based ventures, you are not required to purchase and sell shares inside multi day and you can hold them for whatever length of time that you need.

Table 1: Comparing intraday and delivery

#		
1	**Delivery of shares**	
	Unlike intraday trading, stocks are delivered to a demat account in a delivery order.	
2	**Ownership**	
	You own the shares in delivery trading. In intraday, you don't have ownership on stocks you buy.	
3	**When to sell**	
	You can hold shares for as long as you want in delivery trading. In intraday trading, you have to square off in a day.	
4	**Price movement**	
	In intraday trading, the price movement during the day matters. In delivery trading, the returns depend on long term price movement.	

It absolutely relies upon how you need to acquire cash, on regular routine at that point go for Intraday exchanging, on 2–3 days deferral or month to month premise at that point go for delivery exchanging. In Intraday exchanging additionally essentially benefit and misfortune is determined on month to month premise, yet the acquiring which you can do, on exchanging is on everyday premise. See them two are great, in Intraday exchanging you must be especially master in Specialized Investigation and somewhat educated in basic Examination and inter-market Examination however one thing is certain that you must be especially speedy and sharp while exchanging Intraday, in light of the fact that cost goes all over in short order and inside this time you need to purchase and sell a specific supply of your decision and whatever position you are holding get squared up toward the day's end whether you like or not, so you ought to be extremely precise and experienced in it.

While, delivery exchanging is an exchanging where you can keep the situation of the stock either purchase or sell for 2–3 days however let me reveal to you that you ought to must be additional wary on the grounds that the following day exchange can open up with a noteworthy hole up or hole down leaving you in stunning position.

The intraday and delivery exchanging both are great choices all alone. It thoroughly relies upon your need and prerequisite as to look over both.

HOW MIGHT YOU MAKE RELIABLE BENEFITS UTILIZING INTRADAY EXCHANGING?

Intraday is the exchanging done inside the exchanging hours of that day. The benefit or misfortune is chosen at the season of selling. While, in delivery exchanging you can purchase the offer and keep them for whatever length of time that you like to keep them. In the initial 30 minutes of day exchanging, each stock makes a range, known as the opening reach. The changes of this range are taken as help and obstruction. On the off chance that the stock development is seen to cross the Opening Reach high, at that point it is fitting to purchase. Thus, you can sell when stock development is seen beneath the Opening Extent low. This system can give you steady benefits whenever finished with order, legitimate appraisal of the market execution and ideal utilization of indicators.

Favourable circumstances and Hindrances

There are many points of interest of Intraday Exchanging, the greatest one being that you are

46

permitted to purchase shares without paying the maximum of the offers (Paying just the edge cash). The producers of market permit you pay just a piece of the cost to hold the offers. In this way, you can acquire by contributing less. In any case, this implies your misfortunes would be higher too.

Intraday exchanging likewise enables you to short sell the offers, selling offers even before getting them (however purchasing before market closes). This is one advantage that can give you benefit notwithstanding when the cost of the offer is certain to fall. The business for intraday exchanging is consistently lower than that for delivery exchanging.

Probably the greatest drawback of intraday exchanging is the time allotment. Regardless of how sure you will be, you need to sell the offers inside multi day. Along these lines, if the offer loses value, you are certain to lose cash as well. You additionally don't get the advantages of long haul speculation like profits, rewards and so forth in intraday exchanging. Another negative part of intraday exchanging is that it can turn out to be very unpleasant as you have to screen the business sectors ceaselessly. Also, with day by day benefits and misfortunes, it can negatively affect a dealer's psychological prosperity.

SELECTION CHOICE BETWEEN INTRADAY AND DELIVERY EXCHANGING, WHICH ONE'S BETTER FOR YOU?

Shockingly, the pull of speedy cash sucks in financial specialists who ought to preferably avoid intraday exchanging. Intraday dealers purchase shares for only couple of minutes or hours though delivery brokers may purchase for quite a long time or years.

Presently on the off chance that you, as an intraday merchant can pass judgment on the state of mind of offer costs at standard, little interims, at exactly that point should you consider intraday exchanging. You should be great at specialized investigation. There are numerous specialized apparatuses that likewise help in anticipating momentary offer value developments.

CHAPTER FIVE
FUNDAMENTAL / TECHNICAL ANALYSIS

Analysis of investment includes evaluating the potential investments and recognizing interesting protections and resources. The value of investment shows the value that financial specialists would pay for the investment if that they had a total comprehension of the investment's characteristics. A generally utilized way to deal with evaluating the analysis of an investment is to assess the present estimation of all the money streams that the investment will create later on. There has consistently been a distinction of conclusion over strategies for investigation in financial exchanges. These sentiments are generally outrageous considerations.

FUNDAMENTAL ANALYSIS

Dynamic administrators frequently attempt to recognize and catch market inadequacies through fundamental analysis. For value speculators, this procedure means directing an intensive investigation of an organization's plan of action, its prospects, and its monetary circumstance. This investigation may include meeting organization the board and talking them about their methodology and the possibilities of the organization. Experts must take care not to damage laws and guidelines when social occasion data. They will likely distinguish organizations that have preferable prospects over the financial exchange cost reflects. Ordinarily, an investigator or venture chief plays out some type of central examination to land at an expected an incentive for an organization's offers. On the off chance that the offer cost is essentially underneath the assessed worth, the chief will build the weighting of the offers in the portfolio or add the offers to the portfolio.

The estimation of a security can be seen as the present value of all the money streams the security will produce later on. For instance, if you assume that financial specialists can appraise the estimation of a stock by limiting every one of the profits they hope to get while they hold the stock and including the returns from selling the stock. Value that is evaluated along these lines is referred to as fundamental analysis.

Although fundamental values are not discernible, numerous dynamic venture chiefs endeavor to precisely assess them. Managers are utilizing fundamental analysis on the reason that security market costs will in general push toward their evaluations of principal esteems. They can create remarkable returns when they precisely gauge esteems and make the fitting ventures before other market members. To assess basic qualities, they should figure future money streams and gauge the rates at which these money streams are limited. Supervisors utilizing key examination consider numerous issues when shaping venture sentiments. The issues most essential to their sentiments fluctuate as per the sort of advantage they are investigating. For instance, when investigating fixed-pay protections, (for example, bonds, notes, and bills), chiefs think about borrower's capacity and ability to pay their obligations that is, borrower's financial soundness and dependability. Loan specialists believe borrowers to be reliable on the off chance that they expect that the borrowers will most likely pay interest, head, and favored profits when due. They believe borrowers to be dependable on the off chance that they expect that borrowers will orchestrate their issues to guarantee that they can and will make these installments.

TECHNICAL ANALYSIS

Authorities utilizing technical analysis study showcase data, including value examples and exchanging volumes, while administrators utilizing social investigation center around pointers of market notion, for example, maker's new requests or lists of buyer desires. Some investment directors utilize a specialized methodology, looking to survey cost and exchanging volume inclines in the securities exchange to distinguish shares that may beat or fail to meet expectations. For instance, a functioning director who trusts in energy will attempt to put resources into offers that have as of late been ascending in the market, which depends on the idea that a rising offer will keep on rising. Different supervisors may search for indications of imbalance between the potential purchasers and dealers of an offer to attempt to anticipate which heading the offer is probably going to move. Review from the talk about free market activity in the Microeconomics part that an expansion sought after or a lessening in supply will ordinarily make costs increment. So also, a diminishing sought after or an expansion in supply will commonly make costs decline. Investment directors who utilize specialized and social methodologies attempt to purchase a specific security or resource before any incline in purchaser's interest or a decline in vender's interest makes the cost of the security rise, and they attempt to sell before an expansion in dealer intrigue or a decline in purchaser's interest makes the cost of the security fall.

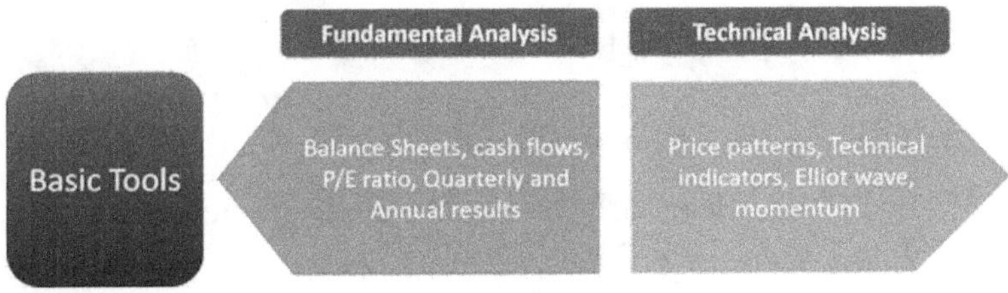

WHY SHOULD YOU USE FUNDAMENTAL AND TECHNICAL ANALYSIS?

Managers think about monetary information and past obtaining narratives to decide if borrowers are financially sound and dependable. When breaking down values, they give close consideration to a backer's future prospects for winning cash and creating important resources. Among numerous different issues, they think about the accompanying:

- Interest for the organization's items and the cost of delivering those items

- Quality, soundness, and security of the organization's administration, workforce, and physical and scholarly resources

- Measure of obligation the organization uses to support its tasks and ventures

- Estimation of choices to suspend or extend activities or to participate in new activities

- Prospects for problematic mechanical advancements, the burden or evacuation of critical administrative limitations, and legitimate or extra-lawful seizures that may influence the organization's reasonability

- Macroeconomic issues, for example, prospects for swelling, national monetary development, and joblessness

- Lawful and administrative condition the

organization works inside and whether any real changes are arranged

- Corporate administration issues that may enable corporate chiefs to waste or abuse corporate income that generally could be disseminated to investors or be held to satisfy obligation holders

When analyzing elective speculations, the issues considered will likewise vary. For instance, when dissecting land ventures, chiefs think about how the estimation of the property contrasts and comparative properties in the territory, how its rental prospects may create later on, and whether there is extension to increase the value of the property through redevelopment. Chiefs utilizing essential examination consider the particular factors that are required to influence the estimation of the sort of benefit being investigated.

Choice of Investor

You can feel every one of these sentiments is too extraordinary to even consider. Nothing in this world is completely futile and nothing on the planet is splendidly valuable. You also have your assessments on both the strategies for analysis. Here are a few considerations regarding the matter both Fundamental Analysis and Technical Analysis have their very own focal points and burdens.

- It relies upon you-which one (strategy) suits your style of contributing/exchanging.

- It additionally relies upon your 'kind of character'.

- It relies upon what qualities you have. Take a brain test to comprehend whether you are left brained or right brained.

- It relies upon whether you are a dealer or a financial specialist.

- It likewise relies upon whether you are short, medium or long haul merchant/speculator.

While there is not a viable alternative for fundamental analysis with regards to the correct valuation of scrip. There is not a viable replacement for technical analysis with regards to the best hazard the executive's device over a brief timeframe. To finish up, you feel the discussion between the Fundamental Analysis and Technical Analysis is unjustified. Analysis must be apple to apple and not apple to oranges.

CHAPTER SIX
WHEN TO BUY AND WHEN TO SELL

Being able to buy at right time and sell at right time can make profit for you. For that you need to do your own research: study financial statements, industrial aspects, and economic situation, watch news and keep yourself updated by subscribing analysts services for several companies and industries.

BUYING AND SELLING – THE FUNDAMENTALISTS

Fundamentalists use discounted cash flow techniques and earnings multiplier approach to value a common stock.

Discounted cash flow technique applies present value concepts to determine the value of a stock (intrinsic value). For instance, dividend discount model is used to forecast the dividends expected to receive throughout the life of a stock. These dividends are discounted back to the present by using an appropriate rate of return (required rate of return by an investor) and added.

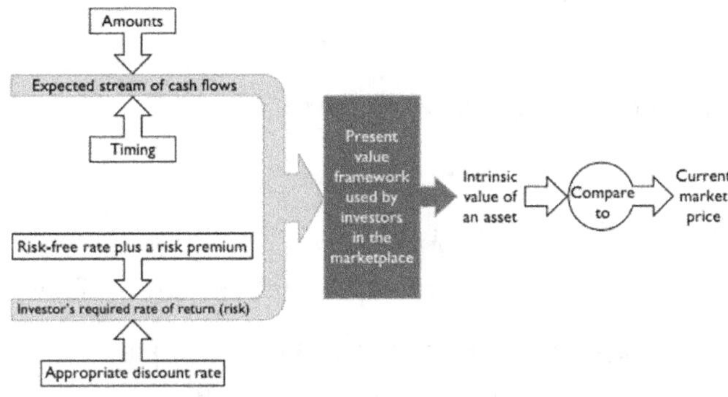

Figure 7 Using Present Value to find intrinsic value.

Source: Investments by Charles P. jones, 12th ed., "Chapter 10"

The earnings multiplier method aims projected earnings and a multiplier, the P/E ratio to arrive at estimated intrinsic value.

Both of these techniques yield a same result – an estimated or intrinsic value of the stock also called its "fair value".

- The estimated or anticipated value of a stock is simple what an investor believes a stock worth is called **intrinsic value.**

- A typical practitioner approach to valuation, however, relies on dividend discount model as a basics to valuation to stock.

Intrinsic value vs. market value

Value of security at which it is trading in the market right now is called **current market value**. There is a relationship among intrinsic value of a stock (IV) and its current market price (CMP). This relationship is very important as it generate buying and selling signals for an investor.

Particularly,

- If intrinsic value of a stock is greater than current market price of the stock, the asset is considered under-valued. In this case, an investor should **buy** the stock or hold it if already owned.

- If intrinsic value of a stock is less than its current market price, the asset is over-valued and should not be bought. In this case, an investor should **sell** the stock if already held.

- If intrinsic value of a stock is equal to current

market value of a stock, the asset is fairly valued. In this case, an investor should neither buy nor sell the stock.

Security analysts therefore quest for undervalued or overvalued stocks by simply calculating the intrinsic value of the stock and then collate this value to the current market price of the stock. Usually, stocks are not fairly valued, thereby carry off buy or sell opportunity.

Nevertheless, calculating intrinsic value is an art not science and because of that it is always subject to error.

A wise investor base its decision of buying and selling on considerable differences in estimated (intrinsic) value vs. current market value. For example, if you calculate the intrinsic value of Apple stock at $200 and it is selling for $197 (as at August 7, 2019), then the difference is not much significant. But after a careful analysis you have calculated the intrinsic value for Apple at $200 when it is selling for $150, then the difference here is much significant and you should buy the stock because it is under-valued. In the same manner, your prudent analysis suggests an intrinsic value of $125 when it is selling at $197, you should not buy the stock and in fact sell the stock if already held because it is over-valued.

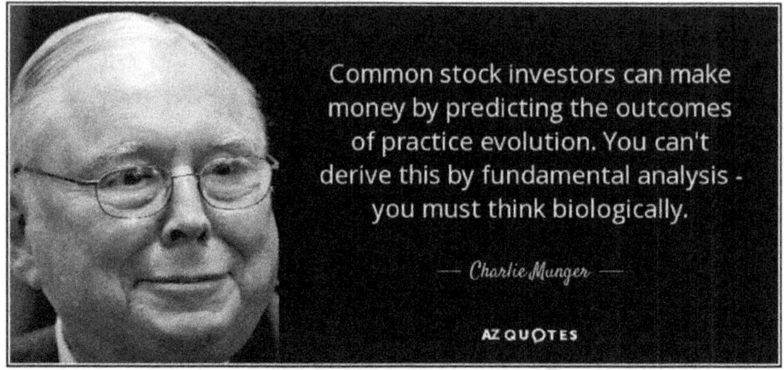

BUYING AND SELLING – TECHNICIANS

Dating back to 1980s technical analysis approach to selection of common stock is the oldest and controversial. This is considered as ineffective yet considered productive by many investors.

- *Technical analysis typically relies on explicit market data for the analysis of stock prices collectively and individually.*

Market data involves information for stock prices and volumes. Analysts who rely on technical analysis for the selection of stocks are called technicians. Technicians tries to access the factors affecting stocks through technical indicators, like market sentiments, breadth-of-market data, momentum and other indicators.

As discussed in the previous chapter that technicians charts and graphs to determine the stock princes trends and behaviour. These trends provide useful information for trading (buying and selling) decisions.

Moving averages

It is one of the methods adopted by technicians to discern stock price trends. At first, a period is decided over which a moving average is to be calculated. After that a fresh value of moving average is calculated by skipping the initial value and adding the most recent one. This process is performed over and over again on daily (or weekly) basis to obtain a moving average line which signifies the stock prices behaviour.

Moving average vs. current market price

Moving average, when compared with current market price of the stock, yields buy or sell signals.

- When current market price is rise above moving average, a **buy** signal is generated.

- When current market price remains below moving average, a **sell** signal is generated.

Price Charts

Due to lack of evidence, it is impossible to provide any conclusion on the basis of charts and graphs. However, this is still used by many technicians for the analysis and interpretation of stock prices trends.

Relative Strength Index (RSI)

The most common momentum indicator used in technical analysis is RSI. It has a range between 0 and 100. Normally, its range is set between 20 and 80 or 30 and 70. It is measured by two lines i.e. K line and the D line. Both have formula to calculate which are not discussed here because it is out of the scope of this book. Its K line that indicates the major signals in the chart.

- If the value of RSI drops below 50 and then back above it, a **buy** signal is generated.

- If the value of RSI rise above 50 and then back below it, a **sell** signal is generated.

Figure 8 Trading signals using RSI

WHICH ONE TO RELY?

Well! That really matters because two approaches yield different results. It is said that if you are new to investment and seeking profit in short term, use technical analysis for the selection of stocks. But if you are aiming at long term investment, then rely on fundamental analysis.

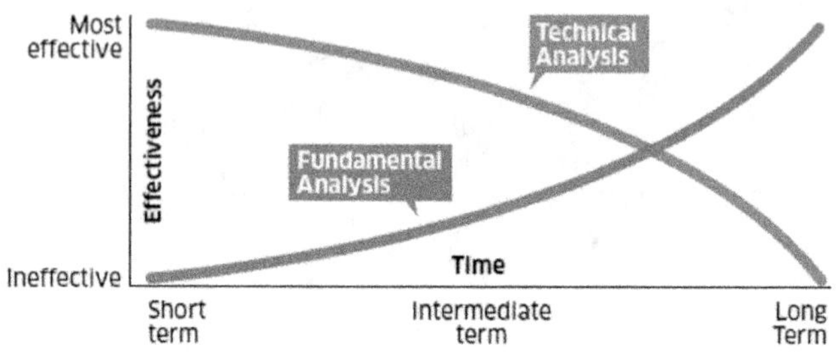

Most effective
Ineffective
Effectiveness
Technical Analysis
Fundamental Analysis
Time
Short term
Intermediate term
Long Term

CHAPTER SEVEN
RETURN EXPECTATIONS AND COMPARISON

An investment decision involves around the calculations of **return** on investment over the defined period of time. A good investment decision yield relatively significant returns at the given level of **risk**. Therefore, the fundamental concepts governing investment decision includes return and risk.

There is no such thing as high returns without risk.
~ Gerry Schwartz

Why do people invest?

Every investor has a hope to get something "extra"

while doing investment. This extra is called return and becomes the opportunity cost. By holding the cash in any form, one may forgo the opportunity to earn a return on that cash. Furthermore, inflation erode the purchasing power of cash.

RETURNS

Anticipation of return vs. realization of return

Investors aim to yield higher return for the future by investing today, forming an expectation for the return over some future period. However, realized return (actual return over some past period) may be different. In the end, investors are left with realized returns. This means that investors' actual return on their investment end up being above or below than their anticipated return. This is the nature of every investment process: the risk component of each investment is always taken into account by investors.

The components of return

Typically, there are two components of asset returns:

- **Yield**

Investment in assets is done to generate constant cash flows (called income) in the form of dividends (from shares) and interest (from bonds). Yield is defined as measurement of cash flow of a security in comparison to its market price or purchase price.

- **Capital gain (loss)**

Capital gain (or loss) is defined as appreciation (or depreciation) in the price of the asset. It is simply the difference between current market price and purchase price of a security. If this difference is positive, it is called capital gain; if this difference is negative, it is called capital loss.

Adding both components

The total return is calculated by putting the two components together:

$$Total\ return = Yield + Capital\ Gain\ (or\ loss)$$

Where yield is the income part and capital gain (or loss) results from price fluctuations of a security.

Example – Calculation of total return over a period of 5 years

Assume that you have invested in a stock A of a hypothetical company ABC for the period of 5 years, which now has been ended. Consider this stock has a price of $20 at year 0. The annual prices of this stock along with the dividends are as given in table 1:

Table 2: Stock A prices and yields

Years	Price ($)	Dividend ($)
1	25	1
2	30	2
3	28	2
4	40	4
5	36	3

Had you sold the stock at the end of year 1, the total return would have been:

$$Total\ return = Yield + Capital\ Gain\ (or\ loss)$$

$$Total\ return = 1 + (25 - 20)$$

$$Total\ return = 1 + 5$$

$$Total\ return = \$6$$

The return on investment in terms of percentage in year 1, can be calculated as:

$$\%\ Total\ return = \frac{6}{20}\ x\ 100$$

$$\%\ Total\ return = 30\%$$

Similarly, total return and percentage total return for the following years can be calculated, as depicted in the table 2.

Table 3: Calculations of total return and percentage total return

Years	Price ($)	Dividend ($)	Total return	% Total return
1	25	1	6	30%
2	30	2	7	28%
3	28	2	0	0%
4	40	4	16	57%
5	36	3	(1)	(2.5%)

Using arithmetic mean, the average annual return on this investment over the period of 5-years is calculated from the following formula:

$$\bar{X} = \frac{\Sigma X}{n}$$

$$\bar{X} = \frac{30\% + 28\% + 0\% + 57\% - 2.5\%}{5}$$

$$\bar{X} = 22.5\%$$

Another popular method of measuring average annual return is geometric mean:

$$GM = [(1+TR_1)(1+TR_2)\ldots\ldots (1+TR_n)]^n - 1$$

Where,

GM = Geometric mean

TR= is the series of total return in fractions

n = number of years

Comparing annual average returns of two stocks

If we hold the risks each of given stock being constant, average annual return yield by stock A and stock B over the period of 5-years are given under:

Table 4: Comparing annual average returns

Stocks	Average annual returns
Stock A	22.5%
Stock B	20.0%

Which of these would you prefer? Obviously, stock A – the one offering more returns on your investment.

How to calculate expected returns?

All our discussion from previous section revolves

around the returns gain from the past data. However, you are about to take decision for potential (expected) returns. As everyone knows, future is uncertain. No one can predict the future accurately. In this case, one have to apply probability distribution for a security that combine the possible outcomes occur for that security for the designated period of time along with the probabilities attached with these possible outcomes. The sum of probability is always equal to 1.0, or 100 percent.

Consider a stock X having following possible outcomes along with the probabilities (based upon economic performance). If economy performs better (Boom), stock will yield 30% return in one year from now; if economy remains stable, it will yield 10% return; if economy does not perform better (recession), it will yield negative 20% return. Furthermore, there are 40% chances that economy will perform better, 30% changes of stability and 20% chances of recession. Following calculations will help you to predict the expected return of the stock:

Table 5: Calculations of expected return

Percent rate of return	Probability	Percent rate of return x probability
30%	0.40	12%
10%	0.30	3%
-20%	0.20	-4%
Expected return =		11%

The expected return of a security is, therefore, a weighted average of all likely outcomes.

If we hold the risk profile of two or more stocks constant, the stock with greater expected return is considered for investment.

WHAT IS RISK?

Risk is considered as the other side of return. Investor seeks maximum return on given level of risk. Risk is defined as the probability of deviation of actual return on an investment from expected return.

An investment is done usually because of the expectation of return an investor form with it, but one always end up with risk upon termination of investment – actual return is different from realized return. Therefore, risk may be translated as fluctuations in the values (or prices) of investment assets and incomes.

Many investors always prefer to gain higher returns and lower risks. This means that they prioritize better outcomes and consider more certainty.

Expected Return – Risk Trade-off

The trade-off among expected return and risk is a chief concern in the management of investment. There exists a linear relationship between expected return and risk which implies that that the higher the expected return, the higher is the risk of an investment; the lower the expected return, the lower will be the risk.

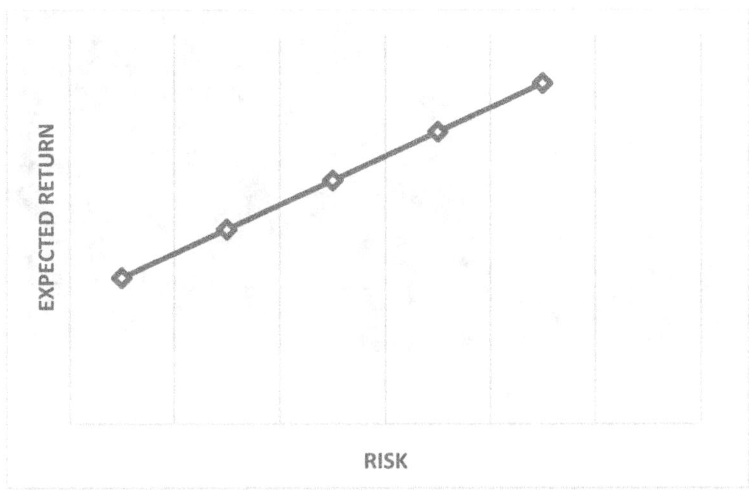

Figure 9 Trade-Off among Expected Return-Risk

Figure 6 explains the relationship between expected return and risk. The trade-off has always an upward slope which shows that an investor is always willing to assume more risk, if he/she is compensated with more return. Although the expected return is higher upon assuming the extra risk; nevertheless, there is no assurance of realization of additional returns.

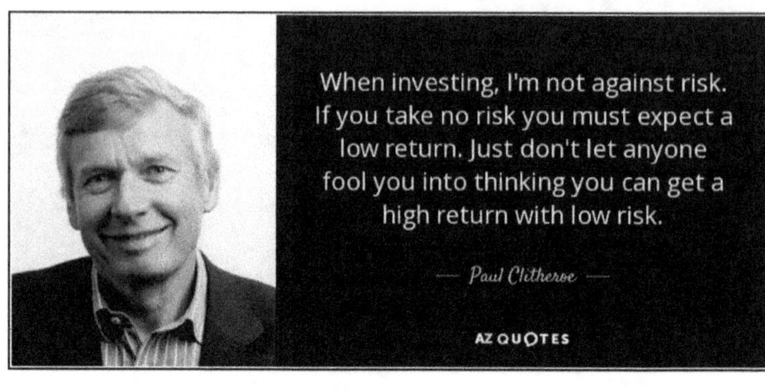

Sources of Risk

The fluctuations in the returns on investments, like stocks and bonds, are affected by some factors. There are some factors specific to a particular investment and there are some factors affecting general economic environment. Hence, there are two sources of risk – systematic risk and non-systematic risk.

- **Systematic risk**

The fluctuation in the total returns of securities caused by general economic or market conditions is called systemic risk. This type of risk is also termed as non-diversifiable risk. It is said so, because it adversely effects most securities and cannot be eliminated. The general economic conditions governing most of the stocks cannot be avoided. If overall market conditions are improving, for example in the year 1998 and 1999, majority stocks will rise in value; if it decreases significantly, as in 2000, 2001 and 2002, majority securities will decline in value. Examples include inflation rate, interest rate, recession, political instability, and tax etc.

- **Non-systematic risk**

The variability in total returns of a security due to factors unique to a security is called non-systematic risk or specific risk. This sort of risk acts on a particular company. This is also called diversifiable risk, because riskiness of a security can be decrease or even eliminated by adding more stocks in a portfolio. For example, declines in the share price owing to negative news about it.

Therefore, total risk is composed of systematic risk and non-systematic risk. According to portfolio theory, the non-systematic risk in a portfolio of securities can be reduced – lowering the total risk of that portfolio – by adding more and more securities. The total risk will declines up to the level of systematic risk where it stops further supressing. This process is called diversification. Evan and Archer in 1968 carried out an analysis to figure out how many securities are required to form a diversified portfolio. They studied portfolio of stocks in 1960s, 1970s and 1980s and concluded that fifteen or so stocks are adequate for diversification.

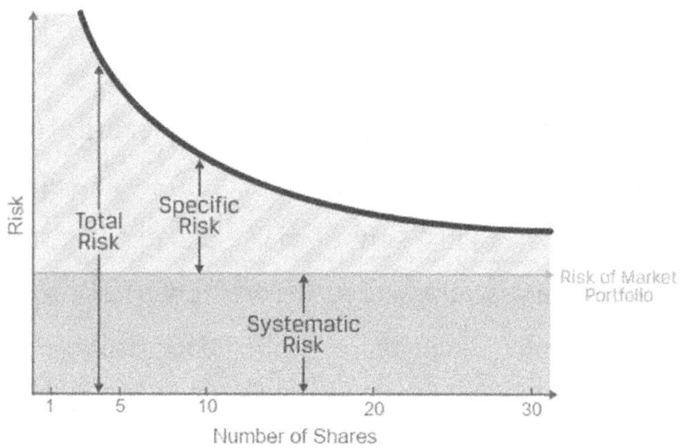

Figure 10 Risk of a portfolio.

Source: CFA Institute Investment Foundations curriculum "Chapter No. 17"

How risk of a stock is measured?

Measurement of risk is considered crucial for

investors. A standalone risk adhere with the expected return of a security is measure by variance and its square root, standard deviation. Both are used to measure the dispersion in probability distribution; for example, dispersion around its average or mean. The greater the dispersion, the greater will be the variance or standard deviation and vice versa.

In table 4, we have already calculated expected return of a security. Remember, we held risk profiles of that securities constant while doing comparison. Now we want to know what will be our decision, if we consider both – expected returns and standard deviation.

Let calculate the risk of stock X. Table 5 displays the calculations of standard deviation.

(1) Percent rate of return	(2) Probability	(3) = (1) – ER Deviations from expected returns	(4) = (3)² Square deviation	(5) = (2) x (4) Square deviation x probability
30%	0.40	19%	361%	144.4%
10%	0.30	-1%	1%	0.30%
-20%	0.20	-31%	961%	192.2%
			Variance =	336.9%
			Standard Deviation =	18.35%

Note that the weightage average of square of the deviations from expected returns is standard deviation. It explains how much deviations from the actual values are expected. In the case of normal probability distribution, the actual returns on the security will be ±1 standard deviation 68 percent of the time while actual returns on the securities will be ±2 standard deviations 95 percent of the time. Therefore, in the case of stock X:

Expected return ± Standard deviation

$11\% \pm 18.35\%$

$(11\%-18.35\%,\ 11\%+18.35\%)$

$(-7.35\%,\ 29.35\%)$

This tells us that an investor may expect 11% return on average from stock X but he/she may lose or gain 18.35% with the probability of 68 percent. Hence, the variability 18.35% is the risk that an investor may encounter while doing investment.

Comparison of securities on the basis of risk-return profile

Consider following three investment opportunities:

	Average Annual return	Standard deviation
Treasury Bill	4%	1.5%
Government Bonds	6%	2.25%
Common Stock	11%	6%

Which investment an investor should consider? Well! It depends upon the investor's risk tolerance. A **risk averse** investor is the one who avoids risk even if there is a sufficient compensation available. He/she always consider an investor with lowest standard deviation. On the other hand, **risk neutral** investor considers risk only when there is an adequate compensation available to cover the risk. Finally, **risk seeker** is a person who prefers risk while doing investment.

- ✓ Most of the investors are considered risk-averse. But the one who will go to casino regularly could be consider as risk seeker.

Other factors affecting investment decisions are age, amount of capital, financial needs and education.

So, which type of investment opportunity you would like to undertake?

"The higher the risk the higher
the return, but always take
calculated risk."
- Ravi Gupta

CHAPTER EIGHT
52-WEEKS RANGE HIGH AND LOW

The information for stock exchanges and other stocks are reported as 52-week high and low prices of every stock. It signifies the highest and lowest price at which a stock has traded during the preceding year. It is highly regarded by technician as it determines the current value of stock and estimates its future price direction.

SIGNIFICANCE OF 52-WEEK HIGH/LOW

It is used for the selection of stock. For example, it indicates the right time to buy and sell a given stock at particular price. When price of a stock falls below its 52-week low, investors sell the stock whereas when the price of a stock rise above its 52-week high, investors buy the stock. This strategy is adopted because whenever the price of the stock hits below or above its 52-week range, it creates a momentum of flow for the price to move in the similar direction.

According to a research conducted in 2008, there exists a significant relationship among past prices limits on trading decision of investors. The trading volume of a stock proliferates once it crossed a 52-week limit, and then decrease gradually.

WHAT DOES 52-WEEK HIGH AND LOW TELLS?

In order to determine the 52-weeks high and low, the closing prices for stocks or indices are taken. Consider a stock reached at its peak price of $150 and trough of $100 in a period of one year. The 52-weeks high/low for this stock is $150/100. Usually, $150 is viewed as resistance level and $100 is viewed as support level. This implies that $150 is the maximum price level that a stock was expected to achieve and investor will begin to sell the stock. Similarly, $100 is the minimum price level below which it will not fall further and therefore investor will begin to buy that stock.

52-WEEK HIGH INRA-DAY

A stock may reach as high as 52-week high in a day but close negative on the same day. It means that the price of this stock may not exceed beyond 52-week high in near future. Therefore, 52-week high level is viewed as "stop level" by investors and analysts in order to make profit. Yet even, there are some investors who quest for further appreciation in price to make little profit.

52-WEEK LOW INTRA DAY

Consider a stock reaching at 52-week low in a day but does not close negative on that day. This means that its price will not fall further below 52-week low in the nearer term. This encourages investors to buy stock and short sellers to adjust their positions.

52-weeks high and low are often exhibiting in candlestick graph as depicted in figure 10.\

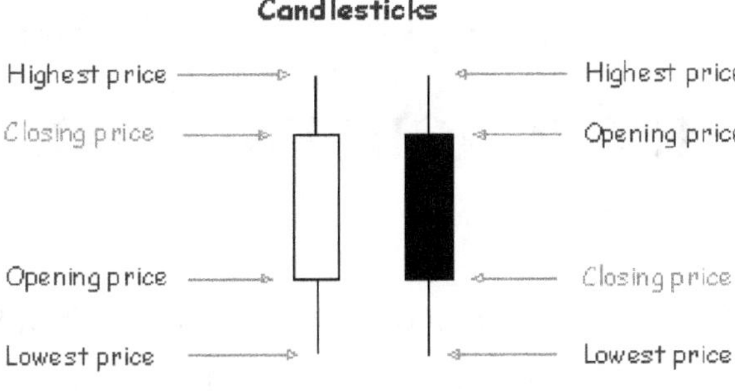

Figure 11 Candlesticks graph exhibiting high and low

Source: Image courtesy, "incrediblecharts.com"

CHAPTER NINE
BULLISH AND BEARISH MARKET – GREEN AND RED

The stock market trends, in general, are explained by terms bull and bear market. These represent whether the stock market is growing or declining in value. In simpler terms, if the stock market is rising persistently it is called bull market; and if the stock market is falling persistently it is called bear market.

BULL MARKET

A stock market characterize by at least 20 percent increase in value of aggregate stock prices or indexes, is called bull market. This market is marked by confidence by investors, optimism and positive expectations towards gaining long term profits. To predict the change in this trend is very hard. Investor's psychology and speculations play a dynamic role in the markets.

Bull market roughly peaks when an economy is going to expand or at peak. In this phase, corporations experience higher level of profits and unemployment decreases. Investor's confidence in the market is boosted because of positive performance of the stock market and the economy as well. Thus, creating a positive demand for the stocks pushing their prices at higher side.

BEAR MARKET

A condition in which prices of securities fall down by 20 percent or more from the current higher level is called bear market. This market is characterized by pessimism and negative sentiments of investors. Major market indices decline and an investor finds no charm in acquiring equities since prices are constantly falling. Likewise bull market, no one can predict the duration of bear market. Cyclical bear market last from weeks to several years. A secular bear market may last from 10 to 20 years.

When an economy is about to experience recession or already in the period of recession, aggregate stock prices began to fall down. This situations persists and causes huge loss to the investor holding securities.

FEATURES OF BULLISH AND BEARISH MARKET

Although the prime indicator of bearish and bullish market is the movement of stock prices, yet there are some feature that an investor should have a knowledge of. These features are explained below:

Securities' demand and supply

There is a strong demand of securities in bull market. Number of investors who are willing to buy securities are more than the number of investors who are willing to sell. This mark limited supply of securities as well. As a result of this, stock prices spike up. As appose to this, supply of securities is increased in case of bearish market. This decreases demand relatively causing the prices of stock to go down.

Investor's behaviour

Investors perceive things according to their own understandings and behave accordingly. Also market behaviour is adjudged by investor's behaviour. Market is composed of human beings who have very limited capabilities of processing information and thus subject to commit mistakes. They often depends upon the analysis and opinion made by financial analysts, brokers and news agency. Therefore, they do not act rationally in majority of the situations. This could lead an improper decision which could trigger a certain trend in the market.

According to Bernstein, an author of prominent book titled Against the Gods, said, "When human beings encounter the situation of uncertainty they produce repeated pattern of inconsistency, incompetence and irrationality."[1] Therefore, a human psychology can better explain the behaviour of stock market.

Behavioural finance (BF) is a field of finance that deals with the study of investor's behaviour in the stock market. According to behavioural finance, investors commit mistakes systematically when encounter information regarding stock market. Market overreacts in bull and bear market. In bull market, more and more investors participate with a hope to drive profit. In the case of bear market, investor prefer to leave market by drawing their money out of stocks and bonds and will wait until a positive movement is triggered again.

In conclusion, bullish market jiggles the confidence of investors and this impact negatively causing the stock price to drive down farther. Whereas bearish market encourages investor to invest more money in the quest for profit – which, in turn, causes the prices to rise as outflow increases. So, there is a very close association of investor psychology and stock price movements.

---

[1] Peter L. Bernstein, *Against the Gods: The Remarkable Story of Risk*, John Wiley & Sons Inc., 1998, p. 12

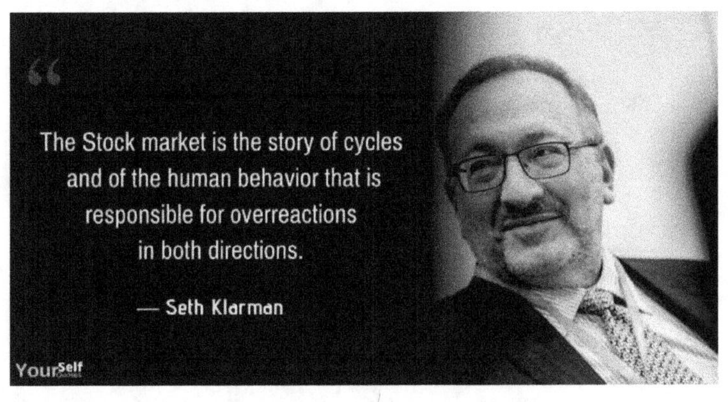

Impact of Economic Activity

An economic activity is accessed by **Gross Domestic Product (GDP)**, which is the value of final goods and services produced in a period (usually a year) by an economy. It is the sum of spending by government, spending by investor, spending by consumer, and net of exports. GDP consists of almost seventy percent of consumption.

- *The periodic pattern of contraction and expansion in economic activity is known as **business cycle.***

Figure 11 illustrate the patterns of a typical business cycle.

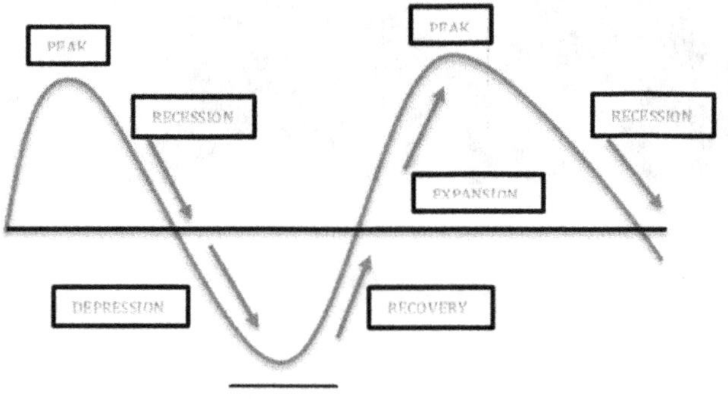

There is a close association among the performance of stock market and economic activities. In fact the relationship is very strong and interesting – stock prices generally lead the economy. Stock market is considered as leading and most sensitive indicator of business cycle. Stock prices usually move (upward or downward) before the economy.

What happens to the stock prices when economy is expanding or contracting? When the economy is going down (recession), it adversely impacts the market, and when the economy is going up (boom), it effects the market favourably.

STRETEGIES TO SURVIVE IN EACH MARKET

Bullish Market

During bull market, ideally an investor should benefit from rising prices of stock by buying stocks as early as possible and sell it when they attain their pinnacle.

Investor should avoid losses, or at least minimize it. Any loss should be considered as temporary; an investor should vigorously and optimistically invest in other stocks because probability of getting return is high.

Bear Market

A trading strategy that speculates on decline in stock prices is called short selling. In this strategy, you sell a stock first with a contract to buy it later at pre-determined terms.

In bearish market, the probability of loss is more due to the fact that prices are constantly driven downward and no one know how far this trend last. Even when an investor is trying to make a profit with a hope that market will turn up, he/she is likely to encounter loss at first. In this case, short selling becomes the only option of obtaining potential gains in the stock market.

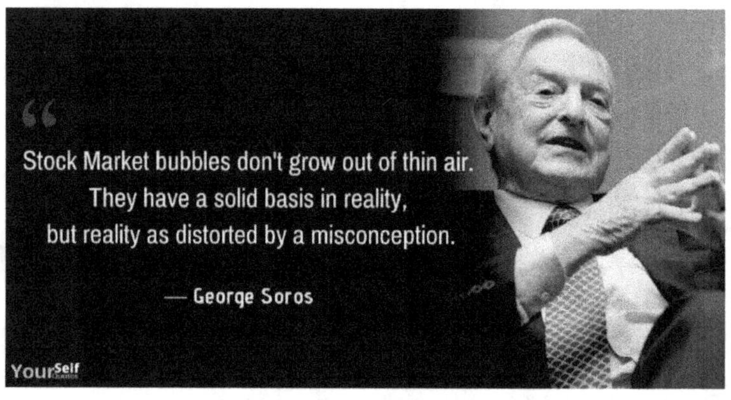

CHAPTER TEN
DIVIDEND/BONUS AND EVERY QUALITY RESULTS

Corporations must undertake decisions about whether to distribute cash to shareholders, the amount of cash to distribute, and the sources by which cash should be distributed. These decisions are called payout policy. Investors carefully monitor a payout policy of a firm, and any unanticipated shift in these policy can bring about a considerable change in stock prices.

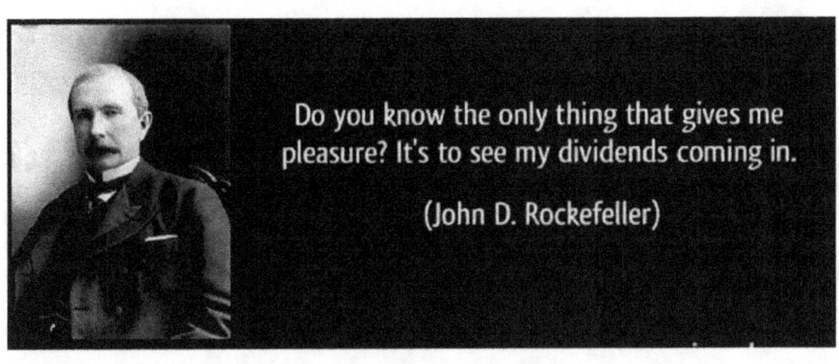

DIVIDEND

The portion of rewards (or profit) distributed to shareholders is called dividend. Company's board of directors (BOD) decide the amount of dividends in quarterly, semi-annually or annual meetings. If a company is not generating sufficient profit in a period, they may not distribute dividends in that period. There are various forms of dividends: cash dividends, bonus, stock repurchase and stock splits.

Cash dividend

The amount of profit distributed to shareholders by a corporation in the form of cash is called cash dividend. The cash dividend per share is decided and approved by board of directors in their quarterly or semi-annually meetings. Furthermore, they decide to maintain, increase or decrease the dividend in any period, and this decision is consistent with the firm's financial progress in that year and its ability to yield prospective cash flows. In every company, there is a defined mechanism by which payments of dividends are proceeded to shareholders. This mechanism typically involves the following steps:

- **Declaration date**

The date at which dividend is declared by board of directors in a meeting is called its declaration date.

- **The record date of dividends**

Firm's directors set the date to record the names of shareholders to which dividends are to be distributed. The shareholders are categorized to as *holder of record.*

- **Ex-dividend**

If you subtract two 2 business days before the date of record, it is called ex-dividend. Therefore, anyone who acquires stock on ex-dividend date or after is not eligible to receive the current dividend.

- **Payment date**

Also set by firm's directors, the effective date on which dividends are mailed to shareholders (holder of record) is called payment date.

Share Repurchase

The distribution of cash to shareholders is not only done by the mean of dividends. Share repurchase is also conducted by corporation to buy some of outstanding common stock in exchange of cash. There are two methods by which cash is given to shareholders in shares repurchase program: open-market repurchase, tender offer repurchase and Dutch auction.

In an open market-repurchase, outstanding shares are bought back by the corporation from open market. The date and the procedure by which shares are bought back is decided by corporation itself. It depends upon the share prices in the open market. Some firms make purchases in bulk when share prices are relatively low and fewer shares are purchased when the prices are high.

As oppose to this, tender offer is a mechanism by which corporation re-purchases its shares from the market by defining the prices and quantity of shares it wishes to repurchase. The prices are placed at premium than prevalent market prices in order to encourage investor to sell their holding of shares. This offer may be cancelled or extended if there is no shareholder willing to sell its shares at stated price as defined by the firm.

Another method by which a firm buys back shares is known as Dutch auction. In this method, firm states a price range at which it is willing to repurchase and share quantity it wishes. At each specified range, shareholders have an option to tender their shares, and this allowing firm to plot a demand curve for stock which shows number of investors along with range of offer. The minimum price is determine on its basis and all investors who participate in tender get the identical price. Following table will help to explain this method:

Table 7 Illustration of share repurchase by tender offer

Offer price	Shares tendered	Cumulative total
$10	500,000	500,000
$10.25	1,000,000	1,500,000
$10.50	1,500,000	3,000,000
$10.75	1,800,000	4,800,000
$11.00	2,200,000	7,000,000

Table 7 explains Dutch auction repurchase for 7 million shares at price ranges from $10 to $11 of a hypothetical company. Suppose, this company wants to buy 48 million shares. At the price level of $10.75, shareholders are ready to tender a total of 48 million shares, exactly the amount needed by the company. Now, each shareholder will receive a price of $10.75 for the number of shares it has sold out.

Stock dividend

Payment to current shareholder in the form of stock is called stock dividend. Stock dividend is paid in place or in addition to cash dividends. An investor receives supplementary shares which is directly proportional to the shares it already holds. In this way, its number of shares are increases than before. Hence, funds are transferred from retained earnings and added to shareholder's equity account. The mechanism by which stock dividend is declared and paid to shareholders is same as cash dividend.

The shareholder does not get any cash payment and yet perceive it as value addition. The earnings of firm and cash dividends are increased when stock dividend is paid, and due to this share value appreciates.

Stock splits

The most prevalent technique used by companies to

decrease the price of their shares in the market is stock splits. In this method, a stock is divided into further parts depending upon the type of stock splits. For example, in a 2-for-1 stock splits, a share is divided into two new shares, and each share receives half of the value of old share.

The reason for stock split is that corporations perceive the current market price of stock too high and this lower their market price with an object to expedite trading activity.

Stock may be split in opposite direction as mentioned above. This is called reverse stock split. In this method, defined number of outstanding shares are exchanged for one fresh share. In 1-for-2 reverse split, for example, two old shares are replaced with one new share, and the price of new share is increased equal to two old shares. Thus prices remain unchanged.

HOW STOCK MARKET BEHAVE IN RESPONSE TO PAYOUT POLICY?

Stocks that generate dividends regularly on their outstanding shares are viewed as valuable for investors.

This is the reason why companies generously reward shareholders with constant – and sometimes growing – dividends per year. As a result of this, companies are perceived as stable financially and become centre for investments for investors.

Many companies attract investors by exhibiting the history of dividends. More investors rush to buy stocks that yield regular dividends, and this boosts the stock price naturally. Public sentiments tend to ascend when companies declare and pay dividend higher than usual.

On contrast to this, a companies that pays dividends lower than usual are perceived as financially unstable. But practically, this could not be the reason because companies might utilizing their funds for some really important projects – like expansion of assets. In the end, investor's perception about the company take precedence over the real situations. That's why many companies try not to skip any dividend.

The company must be paying dividends. Preferably the dividend will have been increasing and have been paid for some time.
— Peter Cundill —
AZ QUOTES

CONCLUSION

It is very important to have goals in your life. Above this, you should have a financial plan in order to accomplish these goals. You want to meet short term and/or long term budget shortfalls, planning for your child's education or preparing your retirement plans; you need a plan to accomplish them all. A good financial plan by investing surplus income in an investment that yield best return over the course of your investment period. According to various studies, investment in shares generate higher rate of return as compare to government securities and corporate bonds. Shares represent proportionate stake in the corporation. When you buy shares, you become shareholder of the corporation. Shares have two types: common shares and preferred shares. Common shares (or stocks) offer variable but superior returns on your investment whereas preferred shares offer fixed stream of income on your investment. The selection of investment purely depends upon the investment objectives and constraints of an investor.

Corporations obtain funds by issuing shares to

general public in order to finance their long term projects. When companies issue shares for the very first time, these are called initial public offering (IPOs). IPOs are issued in the primary market with the assistance of investment banks or syndicate of investment banks to the investors. Stock exchange, a secondary market, is a place for buying and selling of securities. Companies are required to register themselves at stock exchange after fulfilling their listing requirements. This facilitates the trading of securities among investors.

So as to purchase stocks, you need the help of a stockbroker who is authorized to buy protections for your sake. In any case, before you settle on a choice on a stockbroker, you have to make sense of what sort of stockbroker is directly for you. You will need to make a huge speculation into learning and checking what goes on in the market. Prior to making any move, I would suggest learning as much as you can on protections, maybe by taking investment classes offered through a certify program. Additionally, learn as much as you can about various investment ways of thinking. At that point complete a trial by picking a few stocks and screen their day by day changes, perceiving how they influence your main concern. In the event that you can't deal with the unpredictability, you have to make another system or consider enlisting a guide. Working with one, even incidentally, is an approach to get an accident instruction in contributing. The key is to pick up the learning to have the option to settle on educated choices and never indiscriminately to pursue the following stock tip you see.

The selection of trading process depends from one broker to the next. Intraday trade can be considered superior to delivery trade since it keeps away from medium-term risk yet one ought to have better information and experience before being informal investor. For being Intraday trader one ought to be proficient and ought to contribute parcel of time to examine if not conveyance is the most secure. Also intraday trading is the most secure type of venture for example if you approach towards a strong trading framework with sound cash the board. You are out of the market before the day is over. You can rest calmly in the night without stressing over ups and downs the following day. In the event that you are an intra-day or a positional trader, you can improve your odds of winning an exchange. It encourages you comprehend markets feelings. There is additionally a flip side to it. A few brokers feel they will make cash assurance once they get familiar with the technical analysis.

For fundamental analyst, basic examination is the way toward estimating a security's characteristic incentive by assessing all parts of a business or market. When assessing the more extensive extent of the financial exchange, speculators utilize crucial examination to survey monetary components, including the general quality of the economy, and explicit industry area conditions. Basic investigation brings about a worth allocated to the security in survey that is contrasted with the security's present cost. Speculators utilize the correlation with decide if a long haul venture merits purchasing since it is underestimated or on the off chance that it merits selling since it is exaggerated. However, technical analyst use information on market action, for example, recorded returns, stock costs and volume of exchanges to diagram designs in protections development. While fundamental analyst endeavours to demonstrate the natural estimation of a security or explicit market, specialized information is intended to give knowledge on the future action of protections or the market all in all.

Thus, investors and other professionals apply these

two approaches – fundamental and technical analysis – in order to quest for best available option for trading of securities. Fundamentalist believe in the scrutiny of all factors affecting on the stock price movement. These factors are broadly categorized as economic factors, industrial factors and company specific factors. For them, the study of company's financial statements, news, tax structure, interest rates, inflation rates, and Gross Domestic Product (GDP) etc. are very central. Technicians, on the other hand, attempt to predict the stock price movement on the basis of market information. Study of financial statement is of secondary importance for them. They are strong believer of the fact that stock market is driven by investor's psychology. Hence, the study of investor's behaviour could possibly explains the stock market behaviour. These two approaches yield different results for investors. So, you have to adopt only one. It is recommended that an investor who is beginner and seeking for short term profits should follow the analysis from technicians; and an investor who is experienced and in pursuit of long term gains should follow fundamental analysis.

As an investor, your aim is to obtain superior returns with minimum loss of your wealth. But there is always an uncertainty attached to expected return. You may loss a portion of your investment amount. This uncertainty is called risk. An intelligent investor is the one who seeks superior return at given level of risk. At this stage, an investor's ability to calculate expected return and risk could build a good wealth for him over the course of his investment. Futuristic returns are unpredictable and could be estimated by assigning probabilities.

Past data could also provide hint to forecast future stock price movements. Many use 52-weeks high and low to predict the changes in prices of stock. 52-weeks high and low represents the highest and lowest price of a stock during a period of past one year. This is compared with current market value of the stock to make decision of buying and selling.

The general stock prices movements in the stock market create an upward and downward trend; this is called bearish market and that is called bullish market. This trend could be explained by general economic conditions, investors' behaviour and securities demand and supply. If there is a 20 percent change in the aggregate stock prices in the stock market, this is said to be bearish (negative change) and bullish (positive change) market. An investor is require to adjust his/her strategy of trading stock accordingly in both market. Bull market is characterised by strong preference by investor to buy more equity shares with the hope to get profit, as stock prices are constantly moving upward. Bearish market, however, discourages buying and encourages short selling.

Shares are perceived as good or bad, owing to their payment policy, a process by which companies made distributions out of their retained earnings (or profits) to shareholders. These distributions are called dividends. Dividends come in many forms like cash dividends, stock dividends (bonus), stock repurchase, and stock split. The share of a company that regularly distribute higher than normal dividends is perceived as good investment by investors whereas company that pays no or lower than normal dividend are perceived as bad investment opportunity. In practice, however, this may not be true. Company that distribute no or low dividend might be utilizing its retained earnings to finance important project that will ultimately bring value to shareholders.

OTHER BOOKS

WE THINK YOU WILL LOVE

https://www.sriramananthan.com/